BOA
EDITIONS
LIMITED

Diana,
Charles,
& the Queen

POEMS
BY

William Heyen

BOA Editions, Ltd. ❦ Rochester, NY ❦ 1998

LC #: 97–77340
ISBN: 1–880238–69–1

First Edition
98 99 00 01 7 6 5 4 3 2 1

Publications by BOA Editions, Ltd.—
a not-for-profit corporation under section 501 (c) (3)
of the United States Internal Revenue Code—
are made possible with the assistance of grants from
the Literature Program of the New York State Council on the Arts,
and the Literature Program of the National Endowment for the Arts,
the Lannan Foundation, the Sonia Raiziss Giop Charitable Foundation,
as well as from the Eric Mathieu King Fund
of The Academy of American Poets,
the County of Monroe, NY,
and from many individual supporters.

Cover Design: Geri McCormick
Cover Photo: Worldwide Photos
Single Line Drawing of William Heyen: Alfred Van Loen (1992)
Typesetting: Richard Foerster
Printed in the United States by McNaughton & Gunn
BOA Logo: Mirko

BOA Editions, Ltd.
Alexandra Northrop, Chair
A. Poulin, Jr., President & Founder (1976–1996)
260 East Avenue
Rochester, NY 14604

Note

Except for several poems written within the next year, I finished this book in June 1996 (shortly before Princess Diana and Prince Charles were divorced) and signed a contract for publication with BOA Editions, Ltd., in July of 1997.

Princess Diana died in Paris, August 31, 1997.

W. H.

Diana, Charles, & the Queen

The Speed of Light

In Honolulu, Charles saw a king's cape
sewn of feathers, thousands of layered
blue & gold feathers from a species
now extinct. In its glass case, the cape

shimmered within a greenish aura composed
of time fused with the leaves of trees
hundreds of years dead, & birdcall, & for one
split second, his own translucid reflection.

Childhood

At Windsor, this artifact: the bullet
from Lord Nelson's heart; & this: the shirt
worn by Charles I when executed—
still stained black with his blood;

& these: the prayer book of Sir Thomas More;
from Joan of Arc, one charred molar;
the Green Knight's sword & breastplate;
Grendel's evil eye solidified to agate. . . .

Dracula

At Buckingham Palace, one footman, once a week,
spends the entire day winding all its clocks.
Private quarters, corridors, salons & state rooms—
ornate clocks everywhere. For now, in time,

just this flash fiction about "The Savior,"
as it is called: on a secret trip to Transylvania,
Victoria herself felt smothered but awoke
to tolls of this oaken sentinel who saved her neck.

Tsar Light

The jewel room at Buckingham Palace includes
two Fabergé Easter eggs. In one,
a miniature figure paints at an easel
on which is laid an oval of mother-of-pearl,

translucent, on which a few strokes of riverscape—
is that the Volga?—appear. Look deeper
until a sturgeon swims up & stipples
your eye with an effect like caviar.

Sturgeon

The tiny sterlet & its golden caviar—
almost extinct, but its eggs glister here
in a gold bowl in front of Charles.
He dips his ivory spoon into its aura,

taps it onto a crown-shaped wafer,
& bites into the ancient Caspian, his eyes
closed in the slightly-salted tidal aroma
of a woman's body after birth, Di's.

Video Ruby

The great ruby Henry V wore
at the Battle of Agincourt
is now set in the Imperial Crown.
In one of the jewel's corridors

eidolons of English bowmen in 1415
contend in light from stars
in the furthest constellations,
& Henry's sword glitters.

Omen

Wedding eve festivities begin at 10 p.m.
Charles lights the first of 101 bonfires that will form
a constellation reaching to every national shore,
the last at St. Kilda in the Western Isles

off Scotland where deer smell woodsmoke
& great fish lift up to record that flame
in their inner eyes. Rule, Britannia. A whale
spouts blood under the moon.

Peace Piece

A metalsmith in Berlin mounted Di
on his Volkswagen hood—his icon's hair
bright gold, her figure buxom,
her coppery legs sheathed in a mini

only to where you could see honey.
In interregnum traffic on the Ku'dam,
that skirt rose & Di's gams spread
into a bridge to the next century.

July 31, 1881

Sitting Bull, pampered prisoner in Bismarck,
sits for his first meal of culture shock.
He fans himself with a red-backed hawk's wing
while being served with great ceremony,

as if, a reporter writes, "the Queen of England."
White noose around his neck, gold spike
soon to be driven into his skull, he eats dessert,
ice cream, amazed it's frozen in such heat.

The Capital of Malaysia, 1989

In Asia, yellow is the royal color.
Large yellow umbrellas protect Queen Elizabeth
from the wilting sun of Kuala Lumpur.
She inspects a line of soldiers

standing at attention with bayonets fixed.
All now seems cast in yellow shade—
the Queen's skin, her teeth,
four strands of pearls, & the Commonwealth.

Empire

Queen Mary gave Elizabeth a set of building blocks
made from fifty different woods from the empire's
far reaches. When the four-year-old played with them,
she made a bower for her dolls, the wood & fresh-

cut flowers redolent of places she'd revisit
when she visited. Ceylon & Tanganyika, India—
sandalwood & teak & fir blocks un-
blocked when the future monarch reminisced.

Biscuit

Lilibet was allowed to play with her toys just
one at a time. Her dresses' pockets were sewed up
so she wouldn't fidget. She was taught
a stiff-handed wave, & to control her bladder

for the length of the whole outing, & if she did,
was rewarded with a biscuit.
She was not expected ever to be Queen, but,
well, the rest is history, Pavlov, & character.

Bong!

Lilibet's corgis misbehaved with impunity.
All day, those bad-tempered yippers
kept the princess yipping company
& drove nanny nuts. Jane & Dookie

were the first two of a long dynasty
of the short-legged Welch dogs spoiled rotten
during their runs of Buckingham & Balmoral
where someone finally hanged one from a bell.

Carol

Sandringham House encloses 365 rooms,
one for each day of the year. Which princess is it
who decides, over twelve days, to visit
every one? Music rooms, bedrooms & bathrooms,

billiards & ballrooms, rooms with secrets
that need unlocking; rooms of armor
& rooms of silver, rooms with closets
as big as rooms in the twelve days of Lilibet . . .

Pralines

For her birthday Lilibet got a maid's outfit replete
with miniature dustpan. The princess loved
playing at housework & once cried when pulled out
of the toilet where she'd flushed & scrubbed

to nanny's chagrin. The little girl watched
water swirl, her mop swished, tiles gleamed,
her breast filled with pleasure she'd recall
coronation morning when she'd thrice use the head.

Windsor Castle, 1940

The Queen practiced with her pistol every morning
in case German paratroopers started dropping
into castle turrets & weaving their swastikas
to her inner chambers. The two princesses

heard firing from down under the Emerald Gallery
whose art seemed particularly evanescent
as the war dragged on. At night, the children's heartbeats
seemed to their minds like muffled gunshots.

Poetry & the War

Listening to Sir John, then Mr. Eliot read their poems,
also Edith Sitwell, little Princess Lilibet
couldn't pay attention. She must go down, amen,
to the sea again where she would meet Gerontion &,

by all means, find him a decent flat to rent!
All she needed was a star, amen, but with
such knowledge, what forgiveness? She caught
herself dozing. Also Dame Edith. . . .

Air Raid

Lilibet & Margaret follow Nanny Crawfie
down twisting dark Windsor Castle passageways
to their shelter in a middle dungeon.
There, in candlelight, the girls see beetles

crawling in cracks in the stone walls.
Mattresses are arranged in the center.
Margaret finally sleeps against Crawfie's knee,
but Lilibet lies awake as Sir Child boils tea

Cave

on an alcohol burner, & the long night passes,
slowly. Lilibet pictures planes overhead,
black against the moon, their snouts
spread wide with pincers, antennae

threading down toward the defenseless castle
where people seem only half alive
as candles gutter & her eyelids fall
& their cave seems breathed by bats & beetles.

The Mother

The monster mother   descended from Cain
from Heorot's gable   got Grendel's arm
arm of her offspring   awful to treasure.
But Beowulf tracked her   back to her lair

by the body of Aeschere   she'd borne with her there.
He struck at her hard   with hieratic blade
but thicker than battle-mail   was the beast's breast
that raged for revenge   to ravish him

The Monster

but Beowulf's steelmesh   saved him from stupor
until he saw shining   a broad wonder-sword—
he swung it & broke   through bone-rings & bile
& slew her   hated hell-monger. . . .

Then soon he swam   straight up to earthgleam
& Lilibet breathed   Beowulf's barrow
long after its hero   was fired to heaven
long after her heart   subsided in sleep. . . .

April 1945

After five war years of darkness, Big Ben
regained his illuminated face. London
remembered to look skyward for more
than enemy planes. A blackout in the brain

lifted, the suffering English soul
unclenched, lightened. At Windsor,
two princesses woke in their spring castle
like flowers turning toward the sun.

JFK

"Was at tea with the Princess Elizabeth,
with whom I made a great deal of time,"
wrote Jack Kennedy, whatever he meant. . . .
Marilyn crooned, "Happy birthday, Mr. President,"

but nothing's implied above except
even in his diction his libido stood erect.
Anyway, their meeting was long before Camelot,
or he & Jackie met, or anyone suspected.

Double Future Negative

At Frogmore, near the huge mausoleum
built by Queen Victoria for her Albert,
is the grave of Wallis for whose love her king
jumped ship. Divorced commoner, despised

by vindictive royals, banished in all except
this resting place, she was her husband's everything
whose rings, now, ungleam her fingers
in the surety that history won't forget.

Post Abdicationism

Charles wrote in his diary that Wallis
"obviously has her face lifted every day. . . .
Very little warmth of the true kind,
only that brilliant hostess type of charm

"but without feeling." That woman,
ostracized for thirty-three years at the time,
fretted whether—Charles had met her in Paris—
or not to wear a hat at the *Arc de Triomphe*!

Evolution

"He's mad, he's mad, we shall have to lock him up,"
cried the King's Private Secretary when his sovereign
would not relent. That obscenity, "abdication,"
at first a tiny black egg in the British brain,

now hatched into not one but a brood of maggots
moiling their way upward from medulla oblongata
into neo cortex where their meat
might be that mess of shadows, the monarchy.

From Zululand, 1947: Open Mike

"They're waiting for you now in England, Sir,"
King George was told. The King replied, "Well, let
them wait—I'll speak when I've had my coffee
& the waiters have left the room." Lilibet,

noticing the microphone was open, asked quietly
if they couldn't be heard. The King, chastened,
delivered his speech, sat down, was heard in England,
"Well, I suppose *now* I may have my coffee."

21

Princess Elizabeth in Cape Town, her 21st birthday.
South Africa's gift, presented by Smuts in a silver box:
on red velvet, 21 diamonds of different sizes
to ten carats. From individuals, many more jewels,

including, from Philip via courier, a ruby-
encrusted Bible. Lilibet was now older,
she mused, than the number of her toes & fingers. . . .
What was that poem? "When I was one and twenty . . . "

Happy Birthday

In Benoni, Africa, a wiry black man
sprinted after the royal car, & caught it,
grabbed on, holding something in his free hand.
The Queen broke her parasol on him, & policemen

knocked him senseless. But it turned out
he'd been a very loyal subject who had cried
"My King, my King," & whose hand
had clutched a ten-shilling note for Lilibet.

Britain & the Heel of Africa

When the Queen seemed to her
to be wasting time in polite conversation,
Lilibet sometimes prodded her mother
with the point of her umbrella

right in the royal Achilles tendon,
reminding us of the baby dipped into the river
who'd live to drag Hector's body willy-nilly,
like this, over the field at fabled Ilium.

The Death of George VI

In the distance, Mount Kenya slept under a snow-cap.
February, 1952. All night, Jim Corbett, eighty,
legendary hunter, had stood guard against Mau Mau
while Elizabeth & Philip slept. The next afternoon,

Elizabeth heard that her father had died. She walked
in a beige & white dress onto a footbridge over the Sagana.
Her staff had packed the sealed documents of accession.
On the bank, a huge python sunned herself like a queen.

Phallic

At her husband's death, a Queen Consort
ceases to exist. Succession
moves her obliquely to somewhere
in the royal bower beyond firmament,

flesh, branches, bark or root-hairs.
Now, she reminds us of stories read
so long ago that we were childhood,
& the King begat our country with his sword.

Wedding Present

A cloth woven by himself from Mahatma Gandhi.
Elizabeth held it to her face & pictured him squatting,
bare-legged, in Rangoon, or wherever,
at his loom, or whatever, weaving the coarse cloth

to free Mother India from imported textiles?
No, this was a holy man who wove
with heartfelt wishes for her nuptials.
She wept into the gift, young woman in love.

The Wound

The orb & sceptre were so heavy
Elizabeth had holders for them welded
inside the coach of state for her journey
from the Abbey. She decided on TV,

but no close-ups. She tried on great-great-
grandmother's coronation dress & got
ideas from it. She dieted,
& scratched the Duke, who had abdicated.

Unreported Coronation Incident

Then the Archbishop placed a sword
in her right hand & spoke these words:
"With this sword do justice, stop iniquity,
protect the holy Church of God,

"help and defend orphans and widows,
restore the things that are gone to decay,
maintain the things that are restored."
Then fell at her feet a dead blackbird.

Mitosis

Prince Philip complained, "I'm just an amoeba,
a bloody amoeba." Two steps behind his wife,
feeling himself, apparently, a one-celled
animal that might decide to replicate itself

at formal occasions & thus not explode
(the way a snail explodes when salt crystals
fall into its swimming mouth), Philip seethed
in mediums of caviar & candles.

Deadpan

In Uganda, Elizabeth heard Acholi tribesmen chant
this chant translated into her own tongue:
"The chief's daughter is ringing her ankle bells.
She is our queen today. As a seabird,

"she has come to us." In South Africa, aborigines
whose beards were smeared with beasts' blood
told her the secret behind the primitive corroboree.
Again, she kept her poker face & said, "How interesting."

Commander

His father threw baby Charles into the pool
& said, Swim. The baby, who was "chesty," took ill.
Nanny Lightbody, angry, couldn't argue
to protect her royal charge from his macho parent who

wasn't around much. She doted on the prince,
bathed him twice a day in warm water to ease
the often serrated edge of palace days. Charles
heaped his plastic ducks & boats with bubbles.

Jumbo

"I want him to be a man's man,"
Prince Philip said of his infant son,
& not just once, but often.
That little man's man had a blue

elephant, Jumbo, on wheels,
that he rode for years, & talked to,
& asked to pull his stuffed animals
behind him on ribbons.

Coin of the Realm

Eight years old at Cheam Prep,
Charles often cried himself to sleep,
quietly. Once, quizzed about money
by older boys—what did he know about money?:

only that his mother's head appeared on coins—
he said he got some any time he wanted
from his nanny. This was the day's story
which set others merry but Charles bankrupt to bed.

Distance

From the *Britannia*, on their ninth anniversary,
Philip sent Elizabeth white roses & a photo: iguanas
whose arms encircled one another.
The Queen, alone at last at day's end, lonely,

sipped champagne, she who preferred tea. . . .
Here are Her Majesty in London
pacing her second-floor Buckingham study,
he grimacing into the brine sun & sea.

Oak

Often when a boy, Charles checked
his genealogy. Rooted
in the Confessor, Edward,
laddered inexorably by God,

the family oak reached up toward him
who seemed exposed
on a branchtip like a blossom
that trembled in the wind.

At School

At Riddlesworth when she was ten
Diana dove, & dove, dissatisfied un-
less she hardly rippled.
In midair in the middle

of a forward one-and-a-half split,
she'd concentrate on how to cut
the water like a knife to spite
her divorced parents.

Australia: School in the Bush

At Geelong Grammar, Charles's chores included
cleaning out fly traps baited with old meat.
The glass bowls festered with rainbows
of maggots & their winged metamorphoses & god knows

what else. Charles held his nose, his lungs
filled with metaphors of Calcutta or the slums
of London. He wrapped the bowls' foul cities
in burlap, & buried them, & ate dinner with gusto.

Literature as Prophecy

I wonder if you've ever read
one of those Barbara Cartland romances.
At West Heath, they were devoured,
the girls pressing them to their breasts,

& they all prayed they'd be granted
a life like a Cartland heroine's.
By the time she turned fifteen, a prince
had arranged their bower in Di's head.

The Apprentice

At Windsor one rainy spring afternoon
when Charles was twelve or fourteen
he found in the library among royal diaries
& the first edition of Johnson's *Dictionary*

& sundry other treasures, a collection of drawings
by Leonardo. Charles felt like stealing
into da Vinci's mind & time
to befriend him, to study him,

The Genius

& that night dreamed a tomb
into which the criminal two of them
broke into caskets with knives & scalpels
that laced & parceled flesh while

the master drew. Charles held a candle
for this illuminate whose eyes spiralled light
from the thirtieth century. Even the dead
sat up in wonder & applauded.

Birnham Wood

The Prince is walking. From rooftops,
sharpshooters protect him, plainclothes police
mingle among the crowd. Manholes are sealed,
& acetylene helicopters hover whose guns

could defoliate an acre of forest
in the blink of time as brief as that between
1282 when Edward I conquered Wales
& built Caernarvon Castle, & now, this propitious day.

The Midas Touch

Along the way to learning to deal graciously
with ordinary folk, Charles was invested
His Royal Highness Prince of Wales, etc.
His mother placed a diamond- & emerald-set

coronet on his head, girded him with a sword,
slipped a gold ring onto his twenty-year-old finger,
wedged a gold rod into his hand.
"Have you come far?" he'd touch a subject, etc.

The Daydreamer

Diana stares into a crystal ball lit
with the whole gorgeous spectrum,
a bird of paradise whose tail . . .
or is it a chameleon

basking beside a prism?
So much color from white light
she can almost taste it: pastel
penny candies when she was a girl.

Opera for Opera's Sake

Gifts had always concluded an evening out
with the Prince of Wales. Charles's predecessor
drew on accounts with Cartier & Van Cleef
to reward his women, but Charles's dates received,

at best, a bouquet. His frugal mother
once apprised him of the fact that "Dog leads
cost money!" He'd not forgotten. Young women
had better enjoy the royal box & Puccini.

Kindred Spirits

Little Lady Di had a stuffed hippo, its ears so tiny
she thought it couldn't hear her, but
its jaws opened wide enough to hold her head.
She pretended she was dead, "expired,"

as she put it to her older sister who complained
that Di was daft. The hippo's victim giggled,
grabbed a tusk & pointed it at Sarah whose boyfriend,
Charles, still slept with his teddy.

Postage

Diana as a girl collected stamps,
arranged those sets of royal heads
by year, size, color, denomination,
mint or used, blocks or singles,

or whole sheets, her favorites.
She'd turn to a queen, magnify
the perfect replications, & mail
her future to herself, *Di, Di* . . .

His Story

His story. History. No man had one,
or one that could be proven—
Di's few schoolgirl dalliances,
her few dates for races & for dances.

She'd not even posed nude for *Boobs & Buns*,
putting her, these days, in the minority,
a pundit quipped, as the Windsors re-
invented immaculate conception.

An Early Romance

Di's tip from a movie star:
how to heighten eye-color
with blue pencil on the lower lid's inside rim.
She knows this attracted him

when she first cut her orbs upward,
but shyly, into his. As for him, something had
tingled him—like a sudden acupuncture
braiding brain & gonads.

Prerequisite: The Virgin

"In the flesh," writes Lady Colin Campbell,
"Diana is indeed very sexual."
For some women, this dimension is an entail
of wealth, power, title,

but Di was not one of these. By morals
& chance, she'd kept, as a pubster had put it,
her legs shut—
hymenic admission to the royal ball.

The Diver

Acting out her playbook on flirtation,
Diana hovered: then, certain
he was watching, stretched
& stroked herself, then dove. . . .

Charles imbibed champagne
& turned to others. He & the *Britannia*
fulfilled their social obligations while
this budding girl beguiled his bubbles.

Prophecy

While they were strolling at Balmoral,
Charles told a story to wide-eyed Di
of being in Australia & trying
to throw a boomerang:

it returned & hit him in the head,
he fell sideways into a cowpie.
He & the future Princess of Wales
laughed, & then they cried.

Night Rain

Di listened to rain fall from Balmoral eaves,
the ancient rain of Scotland. The phrase "in eld stillness"
kept repeating itself from who knows where,
or why? This rain had always seemed to accompany her

who once, walking with her father when she was a girl,
dropped his hand & said, "Catch me if you can,"
but he ignored her. This, too, was during rain.
She'd win this Prince who summoned rain to Balmoral.

Synthesis

This night in his Scotland castle
Charles is reading in bed by scented kerosene.
Elsewhere under the roof, a doting lovely girl
must be sleeping, he thinks, & Balmoral rain

must color the background of her dream. If he
should marry, if he should marry her . . .
If he should marry her, if he should marry . . .
His book disappears in a glow of lavender. . . .

Lost Rhyme

Fifty-four matching mahogany chairs around
the ancestral dining table at Althorp,
Diana's childhood home. Barbara Cartland
composed several of her romances at the drop

of a chignon while dining here among
cabinets of Dresden & Meissen. In one,
a future queen sees her future king
in a gleam of rosewood, & swoons dead away.

Love

"Are you in love?" a reporter asked Charles
after his engagement. "Yes," he replied,
"whatever that may mean." Besotted
he was not. Lost in thought, his hands

clasped behind him, he walked with his betrothed
as though she were a younger sibling,
as though, if not so anxious to beget a future king,
he'd rather take her fishing.

Wedding Bells

"The winter of discontent
replaces the winter of phony romance
with the active connivance
of the government,"

said the Labour MP
when he heard of the engagement,
but the intoxicated monarchy breathed easy,
& would not comment.

Free Verse

Charles & Diana together at a reading by the Poet Laureate.
They hear images of a crow rendering gorging vomiting
shitting the whole cosmos, & then recycling while still hot
the entire vileness it had just vomited & shat—

thus stars are seeded into the black void.
As he was reading, the poet pictured a creature bedded
in ragged silks, a tiara spiked with testicles & cocks,
including his, & legs, O those legs, flowing & angelic.

Bedfellows

The word was that in his late twenties
Charles still went to sleep with a teddy,
his old pal & comfort. Behavior
a bit odd, a bit . . . woolly,

but nothing else untoward occurred except
that when Charles slept the bear's eyes widened
as its brain received dreams
of the royal member risen like an ancient totem.

Nature

Silkworms ate mulberry leaves & spun.
Their cocoons hung from twigs like syllables
which might combine to words which might combine
to the one sound or song a princess might sing

on her wedding day. The worms knew the gown they spun,
no they didn't. The worms knew the song artisans
would compose from what they sang. They couldn't say.
The worms consumed twenty bushels of leaves each day.

Romance

Diana lost more & more weight
before her wedding. The bodice of her gown,
though tightened two days before, didn't fit,
but a million pearls & sequins made up for it,

some who were there said. Others, in private,
felt the final effect gauche, stilted,
including the puffed sleeves & the train,
twenty-five feet of it, that creased like Di's intestines.

Silkworms

The entire 1981 output of Lillingstone,
England's only silk farm, was hand-spun
& woven into the bridal dress together with
hundreds of meters of tulle & 10,000 sequins

of mother-of-pearl. These flakes of rainbow
clothed her in what seemed a shimmer
of iridescence forever lingering as afterimage
for those who cream for liege.

The Public

"Totally the awesomest," a fan says of Di,
then pukes & passes out. "Fer sure,
a babe," adds his multi-pierced sidekick with *Roi*
tattooed on both biceps. Goody Grandma,

too, thinks the Princess the most precious,
& dreams can she afford a porcelain
of Her Royal Highness in her wedding dress.
(The puker dreams Di squatting on his face.)

Ours

One day about a week before the wedding,
Queen Elizabeth pressed the jewel room's key
into Lady Diana's hand & told her to pick
her own gift. Di in a daze clicked

open leather cases, perused silk-lined cabinets
hoping a necklace, bracelet, or single unset stone
would sing to her. One did, but here, surely,
the essential gift is the one we imagine.

Chastity

Monday, Charles & his lady rehearsed at St. Paul's.
That evening, to Buckingham Palace for dinner & ball,
then farewells to one another until
they'll meet at altar the next day. The cathedral, stout pile

that smoked & flamed during the Battle of Britain,
will whisper thousands of flames, candles
from the whole nation. The Prince will accept his bride,
the Princess will return her platinum belt to him.

The Awakening

The Queen's Procession moved at the established pace,
eight miles per hour. Her four Windsor greys pranced,
her Queen's Life Guard in tunics & shining helmets—
the stuff of fairy tales—rode black steeds

whose blindered eyes opened into tunnels along the Mall,
through the Admiralty Arch, onto the Strand & Fleet Street
& finally up Ludgate Hill. Meanwhile, in Westminster Abbey,
the Stone of Scones spoke in tongues from Edward's chair.

London

All royal brides must carry a sprig of myrtle
cut from a bush grown
from Queen Victoria's bouquet.
The silk for Diana's gown was spun

by English-born worms. Roses in her cheeks
must not suggest sickness. William Blake,
thou shouldst be living at this hour—a verse
to blight with plagues the marriage hearse.

Lennon

Breaking precedent, Diana keeps her face veiled
for the procession to St. Paul's, & for her walk
down the aisle, & for the ceremony.
In previous royal weddings, the bride threw

back her veil to grant the public a better view.
After the Beatles busted up, they invariably
wore dark glasses for privacy, for mystery,
to stare with impunity, & to think.

Gold Ear

A huge nugget mined in Wales
at the turn of the century supplied the gold
for wedding bands worn by Prince Charles's grand-
mother, the Queen Mother; his mother, Queen Elizabeth;

his aunt, Princess Margaret; his sister, Princess Anne;
& now this one for Princess Diana. As Charles
screws this ring onto Di's finger, it amplifies
the light & pealing bells of St. Paul's.

The Ropes

The cathedral's 17-ton bell tolled four hours,
its ropes pulled by thirteen volunteer ringers.
One, each time he pulled his twenty or thirty pulls,
thought someday that he himself would marry,

have children, & then grandchildren to tell
that on this day he was one of thirteen bellringers
who tolled the great bell at St. Paul's
for King Charles & the Queen, God save the King.

Bower

Charles's ancestors include Charlemagne, Shakespeare,
Genghis Khan & Count Dracula. In his blood,
atoms from the bogs & Roman forums, the genes
of every British monarch except his namesake, Charles I,

& sons. All had preceded his head on this pillow
with his virgin bride, a princess because of him.
Rolling on top of her in this candled room, he drinks
from her eyes nomadic constellations.

Wedding Night

According to my source, Diana almost
called off her wedding. She'd discovered
that Charles planned to give Camilla a bracelet
inscribed with their own lovers' nicknames,

"Gladys" & "Fred." Speculation abounds
that Charles has a "C" tattooed on the royal tip
of his sceptre. In a dream slip,
the Princess bit off a bit of blue-blood hood.

Wisdom

When first married Charles sometimes stared
at the moon beneath his breastbone where
words were merely sound. The Prince courted
thoughtlessness as though she were a woman.

As for itself in its realms past earthly owl-cry
& clouds, the moon kept saying its own name,
which we'll never know—tongueless stone,
barren brain of the night sky, princess companion.

Penelope

On their honeymoon, the *Britannia* anchored
at a secluded beach on Ithaca.
The two huddled in a blanket, their campfire
sparked into blue-black darkness, Diana

listened to Charles's whispers remind her
of the story of Telemachus & the beggar
who'd returned from Ilium after twenty years.
Diana tongued her Prince's ear & shuddered.

Tanning

Honeymooning on the royal yacht,
cruising the Aegean,
Di removed her bikini top—
she was a married woman,

after all—to sun. One sailor
stumbled & blinked over the royal bosom,
& would have liked to spank her,
ditto Queen Mum.

The Huntress

She might as well have come from the moon,
Diana, when, soon after her marriage
she descended to palace kitchens to request
a burger or baked beans. The royal chef

told her in no uncertain terms that this domain
was his, &, later, the Queen reiterated.
Diana knew she'd never be at home again,
so gorged on Frosties & heavy cream, & regurgitated.

Schadenfreude

In Liverpool Di met the Beatle What's-his-name
who preceded Ringo, but quit or was dropped
& forever felt in his chest a chasm
into which he kept falling, past

his place in history, past wealth & such fame
as kings might envy. What's-his-name
the fifth, the lost chord, kissed Di's hand
like a requiem as the newlywed hummed.

Dream: The Admonition

You must never open this particular closet,
Diana was told, but, of course, she did,
& walked in. The Furies, Pestilence & Plague did
not fly out. In fact, all was dark & quiet,

until she found a switch, & threw it.
The closet lit up, & at first seemed empty, but
several rat skeletons in several traps
began to sing: "*Long live the Princess's secret.*"

Broadside

Di has a sweet tooth, as do I.
Sing a song of chocolate, & rock candy rye.
From under the pillow, if you're shy.
Di has a sweet tooth, as do I.

I know a princess, as does she,
eight lumps of sugar in her tea,
licorice & Frosties, then the loo.
I know a princess, so do you.

Parallel Universe

Artificial insemination, Charles was told,
produced more twins. He declined
to ask why, but figured . . .
oh, never mind.

The bulls were right there a few pens over,
but tubes of semen were as close
to a penis in this kingdom
as cows would come.

Game Face

Charles was awfully pleased driving the forklift,
whirling it about until the forks nearly took off
the company president's legs. Too close for comfort,
& the Prince stepped down in a sweat. . . .

Rather like marriage or the monarchy, he later thought:
Get into the machine & make a show of it until
inexperience and/or cocksuredness cuts in half some smil-
ing onlooker. But look good doing it.

Verdun

At a flea market Prince Charles bought
a matte-green double bud vase, made
in America, c. 1914, & called "The Gate,"
as he was told. It reminded him

of his own first war & deprivation
when he was throwing pots, his only respite,
at Gordonstoun. Those crude & cruel bastards,
his classmates, made his life Verdun,

The Secret

& he would not forgive them, or forget.
The bud vase from Roseville in Ohio,
crisscrossed ceramic gate
with two receptacles, would be his secret,

no matter who inquired, as did the Queen,
surprised he'd purchased an object so . . . plebeian.
Charles remarked offhandedly he liked it
(could close his eyes & feel the fire of its kiln).

The Poem That Cuts Through Red Tape

"Cats' cradles of red tape
choke this country from end to end," says Charles.
He's right, of course. Thus this:
a poem pried open like a beartrap

for when the cat steps into it,
as now, you with your institutional expectations.
Steel teeth cut through the feline's collar
& neck. It never knows what hits it.

Piccadilly

That *that* that that *that* that refers to
is *that* that!—well, that pleasures & astounds,
Charles thought: intricacies of language,
corridors & circuses in the mind,

the way words, like nerves, backfold & leap—
syntactically, electrically, poetically—
yes, like nerves in synaptic rhythms, or maybe
more like genes that form but free the body.

Plaque

Ducking into the limo.
Safe again.
Looking out as if paying attention.
Smiling & waving.

One more opening, or funeral.
Or was it a groundbreaking?
Tradition, decorum, & ritual . . .
enervating.

☺

"Diana must conceal her unhappiness,"
said a wedding guest. "The world expects
a princess to smile." Thin as an i
dotted with a happy face, Di

does fulfill the first law of royaldynamics:
whenever out in public, our shy
aggrieved bulimic in her mask
melts cameras made of ice.

Madonna

If the body is itself testimony, is itself
a place of prophecy & revelation,
then what of this princess gorging herself
& then puking into her golden basin?

To what extent is her blotched skin
the papyrus on which, in hieroglyph,
the future of the monarchy is written?
O wet shuddering body, miserable & divine!

Painting

Suffering from one of many nosebleeds,
Charles asks Diana for another pillow.
She brings it, & sits beside him. Brownyellow
light, almost sepia, bathes this scene

in a timeless tenderness—Di's compassion,
his willingness sometimes to be loved
by his more than willing bride—
(as though their marriage can be cauterized).

Coming Attractions

During one of their few good nights together,
Charles & Di retired to a secret Balmoral cellar
to count money, barrels of Kreugerrands,
Koalas, Maple Leafs, etc. They dipped their arms

up to their shoulders in that horde.
Charles told her of a movie he'd seen as a child
of an Indian boy descending into the jungle floor
to find a treasure guarded by a cobra

Fakirs

who wove hypnotically & whispered
secrets of gold & rubies.
This mystical creature kept plunderers away,
but we, lisped Charles, will stay

for as long as we wish. The two undressed
& frolicked in a bed of gems
that each enjoyed imagining were eyes
of snakes protecting them in paradise.

Family

Carrying her three-month-old foetus—the future king—
Princess Diana threw herself from the top
of a wooden staircase at Sandringham.
The Prince continued with his plans to go riding.

The Queen arrived at the scene, & shook visibly.
Had Diana, distraught, lost
in her shadow life, wished to die?
The Prince continued with his plans to go riding.

Cleopatra

During Frosties & cream, Di
decides to swallow a few jewels,
the Pearl of St. Paul, the Sandringham Ruby,
a black sapphire yclept Evil—

& does. She'll pass them presently,
but now, if only for a while,
needs to imagine her body
a mummy's jewel-case beneath the Nile.

Nightmare

Grendel circled   snores of the sleepers
prowled their images   of islands & ice-streams
fens & forests.   Charles feared the monster
but sharpened his sword   whose blade was silver

whose hilt was heavy   with opals & hailstones.
Grendel desired   to gorge & gloat
but the Prince awoke   in another's woman
with his pecker erect   prodigious prick.

Parent

Charles found the birth of his first son
"a shock to my system." He was "over the moon,"
he said, "incredibly proud, somewhat amazed."
Over the moon, out past Orion, far beyond

any possible universe in the non-nexus of Time. . . .
He imagined a bit of weightless soul offswirled
from the creation stuff to form this prince, William,
who mewled & sucked like a newborn lamb.

In the Beginning

When Charles first saw his first son,
he was smitten, but remembered a caution
in Van der Post's *The Hunter & the Whale*:
"a baby an hour old is older than

"any adolescent." *William's antiquity,*
thought Charles, *lost to a monarchy*
time-bound & stale. Meanwhile,
Di suckled William, an angel.

!

At the edge of the Arctic, the Prince ate
a piece of raw seal meat—
whether flipper or flank, he wasn't sure,
or was it liver? No matter,

the press corps applauded him for the picture
& epicurean story, & gave him a 6'
narwhal's tusk
which stood beside him like an !

Art

For two hours in Africa the Prince of Wales
sat sketching within a herd of gazelles,
not disturbing them as they browsed,
moving his hand with the eye in his mind,

letting his lines form & reform
as though the animals were being born
right then from the horizon. But then
shouts disrupted his heart—"Lion lion."

Ears

& then Diana could not watch, but listened.
Charles witnessed that moment of swoon when
the matador, on tiptoe, absorbed
the bull's charge & the sword vanished

to its hilt in the beast's neck.
When she looked again that same blade
had been withdrawn & held at arm's length
to honor the vanquished & their sacrament.

Different Directions

Dancing with one Tongan woman "was like
dancing with several tractor inner tubes
mounted on top of each other
and vibrating slowly in different directions—

"She began to feel me all over with a wild look."
Charles gazes up from his diary
amused to remember Pacific erections
laid to rest with discretion, or whiskey.

Empathy

The wife of the Lieutenant-Governor of Melbourne
        prepared traditional yellow buttonholes
            for the whole royal party,
yellow roses,

but Charles had already chosen
        a blue flower he'd found in a bowl
            in his suite. "I like to be different,"
he said with a grin.

Plastic Mermaid

Once a fortnight, Charles reviewed gifts
sent himself &/or the Princess
from everywhere: crudest crafts,
lead crystal, creatures in lucite, detritus

of a hundred attics, flotsam & jetsam
washed up at Buckingham
to be acknowledged, catalogued,
closeted, & never seen again,

Ribet Cage

at least by him. But today, for kicks,
he palms a little gutta-percha toad
into his pocket. Amphibians, he'd read,
were dying out, even far from smokestacks. . . .

Was he himself an indicator species
predicting catastrophe, canary
in a diamond mine? This toxic monarchy
contracted him to croak like Prufrock.

Is the People

someone like the mayor
at St. Kilda's in Australia?
After the Prince remarked
the sea there was like

"diluted sewage,"
his honor complained
pollution had become
"the in-thing":

The Crank

"When that crank came here,
he didn't have the brains
to tell us he'd be swimming
at St. Kilda's or

"we'd have cleaned it up. Australians
never gave pollution
a damn until that crank
went swimming here."

The East

Prince Charles climbs to the top to touch
Buddha inside the dome of the great bell
of Borobudur. Bell & temple
lay hidden for centuries in the jungle,

but there's a karmic sense in which,
Charles feels, he's lived this spell
before. He reaches his hand into the bell
always forever—jungle, temple, & still, still. . . .

Whale

Charles waded to a whale lately perished in shallows
where rocks had caught it in its rush
among the annual torrent of sardines. A green wash
of incoming tide floated it in swells

& dropped it to the sand. The Prince of Wales,
waist deep in the ancient sea, the whale road,
touched that eye wherein God dwells
in jelly & black light—immortal, undiminished.

The Eel

Diana's masked face parted a school
of blue & yellow angels. She passed through,
then somersaulted & entered the fish again,
this time staying still within them

as they blipped her vision. Nearby, jewel
anemones opened & closed their ears,
& a moray pushed its cross-eyed skull
from a coral crevice like a rumor at Balmoral.

Compensation

With its nose in the air
the *Observer* observed,
"It is not uncommon
for a middle-aged man

with an unsatisfactory home life
to conceive a mission
to set the world to rights."
The ozone layer,

Hormones

epidemic cancers,
the warming of the oceans,
the extinction of species,
rain forests, CFC's—

only the collision
of estrogen & testosterone.
The Prince was Di-depressed & -driven.
God save the Queen.

Lingerie Stowaway

The Queen's wardrobe travels in royal blue cases & trunks.
These are lettered in gold, THE QUEEN—what else?
How many there are depends on the trip's length, of course,
& expected weather, but "I can't wear what's not here,"

Elizabeth once said in a fit of pique; therefore, maids pack
on the safe side, but that cicada was no joke
who lodged itself in the royal underthings & chirped
until its trunk was emptied, & fumigated.

Losses

Lilibet's marriage left her father half alone.
The King with his bad lungs & liver
often lay abed all day in pain
that would not grant him respite. His daughter

spoke with him each morning on the phone,
visited almost every afternoon,
but still he pined for her prenuptial state
when he was her first, her fondest thought.

The Green Prince

Charles spoke to his plants, & felt them respond.
He told them their Latin & English names,
& sometimes stories they'd forgotten
in which they figured. When he clipped them

he told them this would be good for them,
as he himself sometimes needed a manicure.
As he watered them, he reminded them to find
their own true balance of root & bloom.

Global Warming

"Like the sorcerer's apprentice causing havoc
in his master's home when he couldn't
control the spell which he released,
mankind runs a similar risk

"of laying waste his earthly home." Thus spake
the Prince, his words a reality check.
Meanwhile, Di, so chic in public, like magic
overfueled & disgorged, apprentice bulimic.

Veal

Escorted into dinner, the Princess caught
her tiara on her dress.
She bent over becomingly to free it,
décolletage & all, but was a mess

of shadows for her feat
when Charles glowered at her to wait
for help. Such another incident,
so many sutures for her heart.

Campbell's Soup

"Never mind!" she said to him,
& walked out. *Never mind,*
he thought, *you ain't kidding, kiddo,*
& that was (was it?) the rub for them,

the Prince's conviction that Di was dumb
& didn't mind, ever—a blonde bimbo
whose fifteen minutes of fame
would extend to fifty years because of him.

Paint

Di transfixed for a moment by a painting of a bird
feeding on the liver of Prometheus chained
to his rock on Elbruz. Her host explains
the artist rendered the fire bringer to suggest

a Christ figure splayed on the holy rood,
but Di is intuitions ahead of him—the neck
seems broken, & Prometheus's head is lit
with thorns of light that pick up his blood.

Famous Photo

A stiffish breeze keeps blowing the Princess's collar
up into her face. Local dignitaries keep extolling
as Di waits, her collar a royal nuisance
now touched with makeup. She glances

her shy glance at the sympathetic audience
who are in her spell, as though her slip were showing.
Now, as she thinks of Marilyn Monroe
whose skirt gusted to her waist, she tongues her lip.

Mad Sheep Disease

Diana wore a jumper with one black sheep
whose photo traveled the globe
in twenty-four hours. But now it sleeps
against a black skirt, or browses on a robe.

Once in a while, a lady-in-waiting's fingers
smooth it, consider it, then pass it by—
a lonely state of being, really, for a jumper
with two woolen legs & one glass eye.

Polo Fan

"Many ponies bounce around
and throw you from the saddle,
destroying all chances of a happily married existence
if you're not careful."

The Prince was still married
& played for the Blue Devils.
The Palace worked his matches
into Di's schedule.

Watching Philip Play Tennis, 1947

A duchess's parasol,
set with sapphires the whole length of its handle,
sparkled in sunlight.
Do you remember, Lilibet,

those sprays of blue
against the woman's cerise gloves as though
God were putting on display
His metaspectrum just for you?

Watching Charles Play Polo, 1980

A duchess's parasol,
set with sapphires the whole length of its handle,
sparkled in sunlight.
Do you remember, Di,

those sprays of blue
against the woman's cerise gloves as though
God were putting on display
His metaspectrum just for you?

Di Working Out

Bagehot, William. *The English Constitution.*
(London. First edition, 1867.)
Elizabeth had studied it, Charles wrote out passages
including Bagehot's warning

that the monarchy would be mistaken in allowing
"too much daylight in upon the magic."
He couldn't have imagined a bulimic
princess, her crotch public as a photo op.

Communion

The royal couple intended to attend eucharist
in the Pope's private chapel, but not partake
of the body or blood of Christ—
thus to avert, hopefully, a public

brouhaha as slimy as a knot of worms
(as when the Pope in his Popemobile
journeyed to & from Buckingham
in what seemed to be triumphal procession,

Cancellation

as though the Church of Rome had annexed Britain).
If the Prince & Princess didn't take communion
but simply expressed humility & reverence
in the spirit of ecumenicism,

who would object except the lunatics—
numerous enough, but beyond consideration—
who identified the Holy Father as "the man of sin"
& prayed him to hell, with all his legions?

Waterworld

At the White House dinner for the royal couple,
Clint Eastwood was depressed—his latest flick
seemed to him like roses packed in dreck—
& a great white shark

circled above one table
when Jacques Cousteau, intrepid mariner,
closed his eyes to dream.
Charles asked Di to please pass the cream,

Lights Out

but Nancy Reagan had staked her claim
to both the Princess's ears.
Opera diva Beverly Sills
was aria all evening, thrilled

that the Queen had said to say hello.
But back to Jacques Cousteau
who consigned this elegant dinner
to ocean bottom, & whose shark ate the chandelier . . .

During the Cold War

In the Oval Office with Tricky Dick,
the Prince talked baseball & polo,
but then steered toward Moscow,
the President quick to remark

that should the Queen visit Russia, she
must not confine herself to that city
where party hacks & henchmen lie in wait
(like dirty water under a rusty gate).

Pregnant

Di seemed less interested in the Falklands war
than in herself, some said. In fact,
she resented the country's attention
straying from her own condition,

some said. In fact, she fervently hoped
the Prince's brother, Andrew, wouldn't be killed
or she'd be lucky to see one story on herself,
some said. In fact, Di was green, & pickled.

Color

At a book fair Di found a trilogy on the blue whale
by Robert Siegel, expressed an interest,
& it was given her. When, that week, she read it,
a blue atom grew to a bluer molecule

fathoms deep in her mind, though she didn't know it.
That next month, she favored blue outfits
& sapphire or lapis accents,
& the child in her womb dreamed of the whale-road.

Occasional Verse

The Prince asked the Poet Laureate
if he could find the time
for the Queen's Silver Jubilee
to please construct a rhyme.

Betjeman obliged, but with such drivel
("trusting eyes of blue,"
"serene and kind and beautiful")
Charles wondered what to do,

The Purse

but had to let this doggerel lie.
Let the Master of the Queen's Musick
sew this sow's ear in such silk
as flattered Sir John's sincerity

but masked the odor. A lesson learned,
but what was it? Like Plato,
throw the poets out, or keep them busy
"to fire us and inspire us"? Eat crow.

Rumor

The airport buzzed for hours, but Charles & Di
didn't show up. The paparazzi had arrived,
bristling with filmpacs, & local dignitaries
fluttered about like monarch butterflies,

but the royal couple were delayed, or detoured,
had changed their minds, or been attacked
by a maniac who dressed like Cromwell.
Finally, they weren't coming, & that was all.

Venice

Britannia docked close to St. Mark's Cathedral
in the hush of evening. Candles
moved past the ship, script
from an illuminated text,

& the moon washed all stones & wood to silver.
Still married, the two stood near one another
& leaned over a rail like lovers
into that forever.

The Owl

Charles told a story to William of an owl
who watched a princess under its tree
fall asleep. The owl found itself
in the princess's dream, & huge,

bearing her on its back above the sea
for a thousand years. As the millennium
drew near, the princess prepared
by pulling feathers from the owl,

The Child

a handful at a time, but painlessly.
In this way, little (by little) by little,
they descended to an island,
& here was the very same tree

under which she had fallen asleep.
Back where he began, the owl became
a human child, a prince named William,
who must now close his eyes & dream.

Party

The rock he held in his hand had cooled
in the nameless Kalahari one thousand
million years before. He pressed it
into his palm hard as he could. . . .

Sounds of London rose into his reverie.
A hundred feet away, Diana was dressing
in another of her stunning colors. The Kalahari
in his palm ached, & London was raining.

Marrow

Charles read of a system in Ethiopia whereby
contending parties are shackled together for weeks
before being brought to court—hopefully,
they'd resolve their personal grievances

before bothering anyone else. He & Diana,
shackled together for a fortnight, might as well
attempt survival in the lion's den after Daniel
had left the beasts puzzled & famished.

HMS *Britannia*

A cannon has broken from its moorings,
tonnage enough to bust through the wales
or shatter the mast. The millennium closes,
the sea swells, the cannon cannot be restrained,

it rolls back & crushes several sailors,
rolls forward & obliterates several cabins—
how much power will it take to rope it,
to lash it to the royal deck?

Motorcade

In America, Philip poked
a Secret Service agent with a rolled-up paper
& shouted, "Get this fucking car moving!"
The Queen stared straight ahead, quiet,

she who had calmed him down for years.
Bother the delay. She'd be safe here
in this bulletproof limo while Philip
advised this chap to get the fuck moving.

After-Aura

In Wyoming, just once, the Queen intersected
a path in the air where Crazy Horse had passed
a hundred years before. She didn't know it, she'd
never heard of him, but *something* had happened,

who knew what? At that instant, her soul fused
for a millisecond with the Other as she stepped
into a trillisecond's timewarp & wondered
where the light had gone that had just then trembled.

Stew

Di watched a woman washing windows,
& mused the common life of commoners—
keeping the flat clean, stew on the table,
stretching a paycheck, a football match

at the local pitch. The woman's window
shone like an idea, but what was it?
The Princess of Wales made a fist
with her mind, squeezed, & then released it.

At Gordonstoun

Charles threw mugs in the shapes of animals
sort of *sui generis* with twisted horns & eyes
that bulged & crossed, mis-
matched legs—grotesqueries,

but, according to a friend, "seriously
good stuff . . . you'd be glad to buy in a shop."
Years later, Di came upon a brightly-colored maybe
platypus. She frowned, & bit her lip.

Figurine

Someone sent Di a ballerina,
but its back was broken,
its blue tutu lay in shards
in a crush of satin.

Di held the severed spine together
& wondered whether repair
were a viable option, then
dropped the dancer into a garbage can.

Rodeo Clown

Di decided to wear her tightest jeans
& cowboy boots she'd gotten from a Texan,
real shit-kickers
with four or five different-colored leathers

& hearts & barbed wire & lightning bolts
& high-enough heels so that her coltish
legs & ass
might distract attention from her face.

Memphis

Michael Jordan slashing for a dunk.
Di clicks her remote: earrings for sale,
turquoise set in silver hoops; click:
a drunken cowboy yelling in his cell;

click: a preacher wrestling with the devil;
click: American Bandstand with Dick Clark. . . .
She'll watch a while, hum bellhops dressed in black,
lonely street, heartbreak hotel.

Rapture

In Paris during an aria in *La Bohème*,
Charles closes his eyes & feels . . . transport.
The heroine is dying, & this is part of it;
it's spring, all Paris is in blossom,

& this is part of it; he loves Puccini
inordinately, & this is part of it; but
for moments he is nowhere within reason
as dark melody fuses his mind & heart.

Highgrove

Sir Roy Strong described the Prince's garden:
"a return to formality in design
and a growing delight in wild nature."
The poet William Stafford had a cavalier

relationship with form, now you see it
& now you don't, sort of like a spigot
hidden in a bush, or two quatrains
of rhymed verse becoming metaphor.

Mozart

"Outward bound the inward way," said Van der Post,
whose words cascaded like a waterfall
from the unconscious. Charles drank, & bathed
in platypus & python possibilities, & hoped

that he might help his people find the trail
to their own reintegration with those selves
they had left behind somewhere in a cave
or around a campfire. Wolfgang to the wolves.

Architecture for Architecture's Sake

The Prince quoted Goethe to a rhomboid of architects:
"nothing more dreadful than imagination without taste."
They were already reeling:
"People have developed," said Charles, "a feeling

"that architects tend to design buildings
for the approval of fellow architects and critics,
not for the tenants." The Prince's apostasy
was labeled "reactionary,"

Spores

& modernists fumed. One said, "He seems to have
a rather nostalgic view of buildings as if
they grew out of the earth, a view of life
no longer with us. He seems to be looking

"backwards rather than forwards."
When Charles read these criticisms, he remembered
great mushrooms under which people thrived,
& trusted his intuitions.

Gargoyle Pond

The Prince longed for an Institute of Architecture.
Therein, students would practice *reverence*
for the principles of nature, a "grammar"
of construction & design, the sentence

inextricable from its paragraph but capable
of individual expression, a turtle
in its ecosystem, now burrowing mud,
now breathing light under the lilypads.

Lactose

What worried the Tories
was that the British underclass
with their pitchforks & eggs
would forsake their farms

with the blessings of Buckingham
& that royal pain-in-the-ass
the Prince. When the cows came home,
who would milk them?

Marble Men & Maidens

All day Charles listened to empiric hum,
$2 + 2 = 4$ & can be proved—
but knew that the Grecian urn, e.g.,
held more than a volume calculated

by formula, & not water, but perfume,
reminding one less of body than of soul
in the furthest reaches of its mystery
(wherein John Keats lay dead, immortal). . . .

IRA, 1979

Off the coast of Ireland, a bomb
took out the *Shadow V*,
Mountbatten's fishing boat—killing him,
a grandson, & two others. Alive,

the Lord had been to Charles "combined
grandfather, great uncle, father, brother,
and friend." In that terror,
one eye in the Prince's heart went blind.

Impi

Charles dreamed himself between Zulu horns
drawing tight. He & his men
defended themselves as best they could—
sabre, rifle, mortar—but they'd be slaughtered

before the owl could wake him at Balmoral.
But now he did awake, momentarily afraid,
amazed again at how the great shawl
of the unconscious revealed that crescent moon.

Catnap

Meissen, he thought, & wanted to turn the cup
over to see, but Charles sipped his tea
& listened to his host's spiel—
something about fishing rights to mackerel

in the English Chunnel, or stewardship
of rape fields along which river? Where was he?
To stay awake, he tried slicing his pinky
on a Meissen sword, but gave up.

Public Service

Charles read of a Buddhist monk self-
mummified—he'd swallowed lacquers,
then for months nothing but salt water,
then had himself buried, just a reed

poking up to surface for him to breathe,
& for how long? Now, on a blacklit shelf
of the Prince's medulla oblongata, that holy
personage shone with possibility.

Di's Tears

The Princess of Wales wept a single tear,
caught it in an inch-tall crystal phial
shaped like a D, reached for another phial,
caught another royal tear. The market bore

all she could weep, & she wept if not a river,
a rivulet. Nor were her tears a crocodile's
or an actress's produced at will,
but welled up from her experience like tincture

Di's Blood

of iodine tinged with rose madder—
her prince would not give up his lover,
no matter how Di suffered. Next year,
her agent presses her, a doctor

could draw a weekly tube of blood
& poison from her heart to sell
at Harrods. Imagine, a capsule
with their vows for every newlywed.

Toilette

Diana washed her face, writes Anna Pasternak,
"wiping off the remnants of that latest batch of tears"—
Di rendered in such desiccated prose
as flies not in amber but in wet dreck leak-

ing from the backside of a corpse.
For her own & for her children's sake,
we'll let her simply wash her face & make
over the clear language of her mask.

Lonely in India

We Di-junkies see her in the rags,
& lap her up. Clearly abused, forlorn,
neglected (& great pre-cellulite legs),
she's posing at the Taj Mahal, alone,

while Charles is boring Delhi with a speech.
It's February, 1991. She's in mid-plan
to make him suffer for that bitch.
Who drinks the wine should suck the dregs.

In Short

Someone should tell the sum:
he considered her an airhead.
He was bored with her, bored
out of his mind. Who can blame him?

asks this ex-equerry. Her only
interests are clothes & babies, give me
a break. The Prince is well-read,
a serious man. His marriage blew dead.

Jackal

Who can believe the Valley of the Kings?
For an instant, Charles imagines a pyramid
over Westminster Abbey with its dead,
the history of Britain quieting,

the black interior of tombs going blacker. . . .
Then he enters light again, wincing
in the blare of sound, Diana
on his mind beneath the Sphinx's wings.

Verbs

Charles read Laurens van der Post who said
"the natural child of Africa *is*,
the European or Asian *has*."
Charles would have liked to be an *is*,

but having had for so long, having had
basically everything, he'd become
a *has*. But in an England of *has*,
an *is* would have no home but Bedlam.

Farmers

In the Hebrides, Charles waxed ecstatic
on the rural life he feared was being lost.
Visiting an abandoned turf hut,
he was glum, melancholy, apoplectic

that simple folk had left it. He got back
into his car, drove off, & helicoptered
to the Highgrove hut he'd bought as Duke,
its walls now hung with simple dead.

Ostrich

Charles read Van der Post's *The Heart of a Hunter*,
that scene where Bushmen women praised animals
brought in from the hunt— "the ostrich receiving
the greatest of all"—& sang a song of sheer deliverance.

For a fortnight, the ostrich, alive again,
seemed to walk its upright, straight-legged walk
in the Prince's breast, & breathe with his lungs,
& did not bury its head in the desert of London.

Possessions

All swans in England are property of The Crown,
but don't know it. This one,
gray-black in rain on a gray-black day,
floats under alder boughs overhanging

a curve of the Thames. Under her, waterweeds
wave in the shallows. Under them, this gold ring
flung into the current three centuries before,
free for the finding by any commoner . . .

Nature

Charles looked up the Concord sage's first book,
& read: "Every particular in nature,
a leaf, a drop, a crystal, a moment of time
is related to the whole, and partakes

"of the perfection of the whole." Yes, easy to fathom
how a leaf, drop, or crystal is microcosm—
leaf veins, hydra, elemental building blocks—
but mind becomes poem with that "moment of time."

Walkabout

More poems here lately about Charles than Di,
I guess. Going by our book's title, it's a case
of false advertising, but we can't choose which
of the royal couple walks on one side of our street

or the other. (The people demand Di.) But death
because of/despite/for/in love remains
our ramifying theme, & our future seems to fill
with comic sorrow & admiration for them both.

Walt

Whitman's idolaters in England cherish a lock
of the Good Gray Poet's hair,
& the spermful obliquitous themes of his book.
Not even Shakespeare can compare

to this orgasmic American illuminate
whose genitals scent the wind like blossoms,
whether or not Di discovers condoms
or Yorick's skull in Charles's wallet.

Telephone Call

Charles: "I want to feel my way along you,
all over you and up and down you,
and in and out, particularly
the in and out."

Camilla: "Oh, darling, I just want you now . . . desperately, desperately,
desperately." You and I intercept this call, particularly
the lubricious parts, the in & out,
the royal jelly. . . .

Drink to Me Only

Ben Jonson was buried vertically
in the Abbey—that famous story—
but now his bones have broken down,
his skull that once teemed with visions

rests among the pelvic regions,
which sometimes holds true, surely,
for the royals, you, & yours truly when
our asses are where our heads should be.

The Camillagate Poet

"Oh God, I'll just live inside your trousers."
"Are you going to turn into a pair of knickers?"
"Maybe, God forbid, a Tampax—just my luck,"
the Prince lamented. We notice how

it crossed his mind, as it would a poet's,
that the closest he could get to his beloved
would be to be an absorbent maxipad
in karmic use during her period.

Fuel Line

"I fill your tank," Charles gushed
to Camilla over the cell phone—
we assume high octane semen,
the Prince's rigid nozzle,

orgasmic spurts & squirts as the lovers
shudder to standstill. Trouble is,
Cam says, she needs refueling thrice as often
as they can fillerup together.

Blue Leather

Charles was given the first English edition
of Emerson's *Poems* (1847). Skimming it,
he found the verses sometimes stilted,
often obvious or too elusive,

though sometimes their flow of music
caught something in his inner ear,
a gleam of light become audition,
a melody of mind so deep in thought

The Scandal

that all was interfused with spirit.
But then he came to "Brahma,"
its red slayer who thinks he has slain,
its withering scorn for fame or shame,

its cosmic unity that had him by the throat.
Brahma turned, & passed, & turned again:
"Find me, and turn your back on heaven."
For a few seconds, Charles was free of everyone.

BBC

Diana devoured   details of Grendel
who crunched bonelocks   crammed flesh-crust
gulped him with glee   groped with claw hands
grabbed the next nearest.   But now Grendel's arm,

that great goregrip   nailed to Heorot's gable
wilted like wax   in the withering metric
grisly with beauty   Beowulf's blossom
remorse of a meta-   mother to come. . . .

The Wounded Prince

Charles wants his friends to say NOTHING,
& nothing is what we'll say.
Our prince is filled with loathing,
& we must give him sway

to counter his wife's conspiring
with journalists out for dough.
The truth needs airing,
but our prince says NO.

Stephen Barry

"In all my years I've never seen anyone as tricky or determined,"
says the Prince's valet.
"She was like a jellyfish. You couldn't see her coming,
but, my God,

the effect of the sting!" In Stephen Barry's jellyfish hand,
we seem to see a deadly string
of transparent stingers that traumatize Charles until he lies
gasping on the strand.

Receptacles

Jung often used words like "shitbags" & "pisspots."
When you consider it, bags & pots
in these cases do hold the feces & urine
by-wastes of psychic correction,

balancing the holy language of redemption.
Henry James pestled a complex vitriol
into his golden bowl. Stephen Crane,
who thought of his poems as "pills," medicinal,

Lungs

coughed his lungs out in England,
& died pretty much broken & broke in Deutschland.
Lurching breathless into battle, his main character felt trapped
"in a moving box" of blue-coated fodder

for the animal god of civil war.
In a premonition of dead baby & dead wife,
Hemingway's Henry notices coffee grounds
& dead flowers in a garbage can outside the hospital,

You

& it's as though his skull is the mortar
for Stein's whole "lost generation" & their pain.
It all makes us wonder what's contained
within a crown or royal tiara

when worn during an elegant occasion.
We won't mention any particulars here
of place or person. When you close this book,
you'll lock this triptych into its cryptic ark.

Aliens

As far as marriage went, was Diana
Sylvia Plath in a tiara?
Did the two main men
we associate with them,

a prince & a poet, swim
into their ken
like planets on which
body-snatchers flourish?

1588

The Lord Mayor of London greeted the Queen's Procession.
He carried the Pearl Sword given to St. Paul's
by Elizabeth I in gratitude for the British defeat
of the Spanish Armada. This day, the Pearl Sword shall

remain unsheathed as the Lord Mayor struts.
It arcs rhythmically at his side,
recollecting motion, a wave, waves, a sea
of black-green blood, England ascendent, emerald isle.

Upchucking

The royal symbol, John Osborne wrote, "is dead.
It is the gold filling in a mouthful of decay."
Reading this years later, Di wondered how
Osborne realized that when she was a girl

she'd had a molar packed with gold. But now
her teeth were even, her smile at least adequate.
She preferred as metaphor a crown,
blood-pitted since the Tower's murdered children.

Transformation

Leslie Marmon Silko told Di
of the old-time Pueblo world—
how one second Spider Woman,
a little eight-legger,

lives under a yucca plant,
& the next instant is a grandmother
walking along a road. & why shouldn't
Di be a crow, or the morning star,

Sympathy

or a frog, beloved child of the rain clouds?
Both women laughed. Could she still,
Di asked, wear high heels?
Leslie leaned over, cupped her hand

around the Princess's ear & whispered
something we can almost overhear
about beauty & strong women
who save their children during a famine.

Revenge

Some friends of the Prince called for Di
to be beheaded. They saw, gleefully,
her blonde poll on a platter
presented to the rightful heir & bachelor

in Time not just reversed but retroactive.
The bitch had pretty much ruined everything,
so let the guillotine forgive
her neckcurls, & history that wedding.

Twa Phony Corbies

Twa corbies beaked for one another's ee,
& struck their mark. Under the half-
blinded moon they struck again until
they cudna see the night. The fox laugh

to take them at his pleasure under builded
English stone whose tower cast
shadow like a blade—lang, lang—
O the fox sing from belly with such bluid.

Beads

Diana read of "the string of beads,"
an ancient Bantu parable,
each tear of sorrow being
a bead strung

on a thread of feeling
into a necklace worn by Grief,
our sister. Shall she, our sibling,
not be welcome at our table?

Hiroshima

A survivor now bowed to Diana the *Sayonara*—
"If it must be." At the table, from time to time,
the Princess had glanced to her diagonal
but couldn't presume to speak with him,

so inward in wisdom did he seem,
so elderly that a conversation
might powder him to the eternal.
Sayonara, he now bowed to her, & that was all.

Wedding Presents

Tonight, with her beaded white evening dress & jacket,
Di wears that diamond & pearl tiara given her
by the Queen. 1989, & Hong Kong ain't never before
seen nothing quite like her. In Kowloon,

her teardrop pearls & hundreds of diamonds set
in gold bedazzle even the billionaires who despair
for what might happen when China takes over. But
tonight Charles cultures her mind with pyrite & zircon.

Jack the Ripper

Something bogus gets printed in the tabloids,
then saved in folders & on disks
for the cuttings file. Even if corrected,
the lie remains to be resurrected

whenever convenient to sell papers
or win invalid arguments. Sort of like
being stalked by a long-dead murderer
who was never drawn & quartered.

Aromatherapy

One scent was a deep stain, blue
attar of rose diffusing to cinnamon,
bower of flowers to arbor in autumn—
where was she? Tea, lumps of sugar,

anise wafers, a stick of cinnamon
by which she stirred
her childhood back wordlessly through
vapors of pain.

The Morning After

Charles was a tinge seasick,
or maybe something he'd eaten.
He sat on the throne
like a drunk's stomach filled with milk

& couldn't care where next port
on the schedule.
Meanwhile, the Beatles
sang like they were sick, or Muzak.

Springwater

Someone's doing better now, with periodic
colonic irrigations,
ten-gallon enemas not as chic,
perhaps, as crushed pearl & rose ablutions,

but good for the clogged body dyspeptic, guess whose.
During the procedure, a hose . . .
& colors changing . . . but we'll stop singing
the details of royal plumbing.

Acupuncture

Oonagh Toffolo's pins formed a word
on Di's abdomen—the Princess knew it
in a previous life, but not this one.
When Oonagh thrummed them, Di felt

the word like a chord in her as though
a harp were being played by a wave
on a beach too long ago & far away
to remember. *Thrum* . . . that word again . . .

AIDS, 1988

Lady Campbell quotes a friend of Diana's father
who said that "all this jiggery-pokery with buggers
just isn't on." Early, the hoi polloi got turned off
when Di shook bare hands at the Kobler Centre

with splotched doomed men no one
should ever forget. That night, in bed alone,
she put her hand over her face for proof,
& licked it, blood sister.

Di to the Dark Hospital Come

Indonesia, November, 1989—as she holds a leper's hands,
Di remembers that scary ditty from her childhood:
O leprosy, why have you tortured me?
There goes my fingernail / into my ginger ale.

There goes my eyeball / into my highball. Her shy
smile quivers, she leans over this child of Damien
for his sake, & hers. No irony intended here. Our Di,
today our suffering Princess of Molokai.

Identity

Di skimmed the papers for any photo of herself—
who was she? Clamshell boxes filled
with roles she'd become, princess
of the lens, fashion's slender darling, blonde

seductress so demure she must be virgin
even after marriage, after motherhood.
Today, above & below the fold,
she bends to caress a child on its deathbed.

Click

There's a color shot of Di in a brightly-
flowered dress in Nigeria—March, 1990;
another of her in May that year
in London in the exact same dress! We

expect better of the Princess, & these days
there's no excuse, not even the fact
she wore the dress two continents apart.
Everybody & their uncle's got a Kodak.

The Royal Person

In the hospital, Di met Henry who'd
had a repaired aneurism repaired again.
He told her how blood had swelled his abdomen,
& he had bloody screamed. Di understood,

she said, how terribly he must have suffered,
& wished him well, & tried to pass, but Henry
kept hold her hand to say his wife was dead. . . .
Di leaned forward. Henry kissed her forehead.

Poll

Most people's #1 fear is speaking in public,
#2 is dying. Thus, it stands to reason
that at a funeral they'd be better off
in the casket than delivering the eulogy.

Di laughed when she heard this joke,
& at the microphone that evening shone
in her shy way, talking of the homeless whom we
don't want to become—fear #3.

Cold Turkey

You never saw so much red carpet
as in Virginia when the kids of "Straight"
welcomed Nancy Reagan & the Princess.
The First Lady wore so red a dress

she seemed like a gamebird to blend in
& disappear. Di wore white with a red
slip on which one kid concentrated
to postpone (gag) his vomit.

Eton

Di in a tabloid again, this time
down to her bra & riding bareback
on her riding instructor—a dame
in heat, captured, as they say, on film

now frozen into still-shots for a morning rag.
How much more can she bear, Di begs,
but dresses for another bejeweled benefit,
sick to death for herself, for Prince William,

Cross-eyed

though the story is a hoax, the film a spoof
passed off as the real thing.
The *Sun* would do a mea culpa
to the delight of rival *Daily Mirror*,

but images of the hot blonde babe
Princess of Wales spurring her lover
with her breasts & buttocks would stick
to schoolboys' minds like gism to butter.

A Beatles Reunion

"How would the numbers compute?" Di asked.
With various movers & shakers,
she was raising money. She smiled shyly upward
over a sheaf of papers.

This round table was centered with flowerheads
floating in a crystal bowl. *Merlin,*
thou shouldst be living at this hour, the flowers heard
someone think. Maybe John Lennon.

Shrimp

Di stares into a closed ecosystem, a gift
glass ball of water, gravel, tiny shrimp,
a few feathery blue-green plants.
Semitransparent, the shrimp awaken

each day & make galactic explorations
in the great depths of their limitless globe.
As long as the sun keeps filtering in, the sun
with its golden light & power to sustain . . .

Airport Lounge

Someone's talking to him, & he is somewhere,
but not here. The sound of *r*, one *r*
after another, fuses with the sound of *n*,
jet-engine whine out past the trembling panes. . . .

Walt Whitman thought the universal color
was yellow, yellow tinged with brown,
a brownish yellow. For Charles, now, the con-
sonantal color & sound of *r* fusing with *n*.

Respite

Let's spend a minute behind Charles's eyes
during, say, a funeral for someone's cousin.
Through the eulogies & hymns,
we're self-conscious, but otherwise

almost not here—maybe snorkeling Poet's Corner
or sighting down a pheasant in the desert,
or in the Nowhere Mind of moonlight in a river,
or in this pew of amber, slowing, fast. . . .

Elsewhere

At Duino, Charles thought to change his life,
but needed, again, to dine for Britain.
But silverware quieted, a hum of conversation
suspended him in silence, the self

receptive to pure being & the songs of angels.
Twice, a woman across the table tried
cutting her wit toward him, but Charles
could only listen to her wings, & nod.

Lucy

On tour, to balance the rush of formal chaos,
Charles read Jung's *Psychological Reflections*.
On marble floors in reception lines
with chandeliers crystalling his motions,

or at dinners where words were eidolons,
he sometimes felt in himself the passage
of an immensity of time, images
filtering through the gene-pool of his mind.

The Chosen

Charles dreamed a sword embedded in stone
up to its hilt. When it came his turn,
he withdrew it easily, as though from butter,
& waved it in the air, a flame for all to follow him,

but where? The blade burned before them
through forest, along strand, over mountains
carved with vowels as though they were his tongue—
all the night long, his journey, his vision: *Excalibur.* . . .

Relic

Stone, the medieval heart, holding a sword
to be withdrawn, then flourished
by a hero whose kingdom would come into being;
stone, by intuition, opening its chest

to one whose power would surprise him;
stone, a fragment of which, at Buckingham,
Charles kept near his bed, & tasted,
& sometimes pressed into his forehead. . . .

Charles III

In his dream Charles touches his crown
of mud & sawdust. He crouches in the limbs
of an ancient chestnut in the center of London,
traffic speeding around him, blossoms

obscuring his view, their white odor
erasing memory. Is he in exile here,
a Fool, deposed, or still King of Britain?
Dung crown. Bus horns. Piercing derision!

Anthem

At Arlington Prince Charles held salute
through "God Save the Queen"
& "The Star Spangled Banner." He stood
at rigid attention, his left hand

on his sword whose sheathe
reached to the slate.
Three thousand miles away in Britain,
American dust vibrated.

Nor Live So Long

The Prince read another book on Shakespeare,
Spectacle and Narration—
what is staged opposed to what we only hear.
The crafty Bard of Avon,

as in the terrible last act of *King Lear*,
might dramatize death
or might not, each choice serving to sharpen
the serpent's tooth.

Wisteria

In Florence Charles is
overwhelmed & moved to tears,
his spirit lifted by beauty.
He confides to his diary

that great artists must be driven
by "dramatic religious inspiration."
All through Italy, even in Rome,
Florence's purple blossoms shadow him.

Soul

The Prince at the Pantheon in Rome
stands where we once stood at the bier
of Raphael. But none of us is there,
even as we are. Hadrian's open dome

allows light in as it has for twenty centuries
the color & consistency of water
in which all names are writ together
in the mysteries of Time, & spaghetti.

Ad

Charles heard you could e-mail a prayer
to the Wailing Wall. An Israeli company
would print it up, take it over,
& stuff it into a chink in the masonry

of the temple destroyed in 70 A.D.,
"the closest place that you can get to God."
Charles thought about it, thinks about it still,
then turned to & turns his wooden prayer wheel.

Babi Yar

Charles heard that joke about the typical Russian poem—
"Our sun collapses brown-red like a diseased kidney.
Our riverbeds are choked with putrid dead.
Maggots tunnel the cheese. We have never been so happy—"

& laughed. A nation's character resides
in the collective soul of its poetry, maybe,
but who could deny the seepage of joy
from these tragic songs of Yevtushenko & Voznesensky?

No Mind

Charles at a meeting on something or other
drifted away, but kept his posture
strict as a monk's in meditation.
Later, he wondered about the line between

the no-mind of Eastern mystics & sleep—
simply being befogged & blurring off.
What was a Zennist's "active passivity,"
& what was inattention polished with bluff

Audition

after long practice? What's the diff,
he concluded, but kept faith in one past instance
when Amsterdam's traffic was undersong
for ten minutes or twice as long

as others spoke to him or to one another
for him to hear. A chandelier
merged with a conference table, & light spoke
from a centerpiece of flowers

Companion

as though in the extant voice of Anne Frank,
but wordlessly, the syllables never
cohering to words. Charles woke
from wherever he'd been in a lung-deep

freshness of feeling, & no one realized
he'd been gone. Could he, again,
keeping his eyes open, ascend beyond Time
into the tranced presence of Anne?

Prufrock Luncheon at Number Ten

PM Thatcher invited in
a group of city radicals
who had their program, had their spin
to save their blocks from wrecking balls,

but the powerlunch went null & void—
the government got paranoid
that tea & the Prince & the press & ices
would force the moment to a crisis.

Cleff

Before we are born, Charles thinks, Time was not,
& after we die, Time ceases. Time is that
which exists as human measure between
the two darknesses, voids unknown

for the time being. A goldfish does not
consider any before or after, but swims
in its medium as a single note
strummed & held in a wordless continuum.

Bede

Charles considered the Venerable Bede's image
of a bird flying from dark into a lighted room
& out again into infinite dark.
His own soul had entered the womb,

& he'd been born to evanescent revelation,
flying from dark into a lighted room
& out again into infinite dark
beyond even the memory of a marriage

Virus

with body. In a hospital,
through an atomic microscope,
Charles spied a virus so tiny
that if there were as many

as sandgrains at the shore,
& all glued together,
you could not witness it
with your naked eye—

The Bird

moon & star shapes, blue, ochre,
brown, green in patterns of intuition
like a Rorschach satori,
De Rerum Natura, invisible beauty,

Lucretius staring at the heavens
which were a wash of light
into which flew his mind
with hermetic definitions.

Affair

At their first meeting, Di told James Hewitt
of an accident she'd had as a girl:
she'd fallen from her horse & almost
broken an arm. The Captain, in charge of stables,

galloped with the Princess's gambit
& offered lessons so she could get
her confidence back so she'd be able,
again, to sit with pleasure in the saddle.

Menagerie

On his first real date with Di,
James Hewitt wore a Hermés tie
patterned with tiny animals
kicking up their heels,

cavorting, having fun; & maybe
thirty cute & cuddly
stuffed creatures were tucked up
in the Princess's bed—ape

The Jungle

to zebra including several monkeys
clasping their long arms & tails.
Di & the Captain nervously
smalltalked in anticipatory ecstasy

until Di slipped her body
into his lap, & kissed him,
& the two explored her bedroom,
lovers on safari.

Trojan Horse

After Di wept her unhappiness to him,
Captain Hewitt assured her she was not alone,
that he would always be her friend
& dearer friend than she had ever known.

All the other husbands were at home,
or dead. Penelope at her loom
rocked her mnemonic shuttle. Di, hold tight
to your lover's pommel against midnight.

Tank

Hewitt signed his last will & testament,
then went to war for oil in the desert.
Diana wrote him every day,
sometimes twice, & once saw him

on the news in his maroon beret.
The sand was so much shrapnel in her heart—
armour blown apart—
their love a hopelessly moving target.

The Mind in Its Own Place

Trekking sand in the Valley of the Kings,
Charles closed his eyes & tried to concentrate
on the dry dark in which Tutankhamen rested—
not his tomb or a museum, not any particular place

on this our earth, but somewhere everywhere
& nowhere at once. The pyramids floated
in motes of dust from Anubis's jackal snout.
Diana would look best in mummy wrappings.

They

During the crisis of abdication, Margaret, six,
asked her nanny, "Are they going to cut off
his head?" In essence, of course, they did,
though the body took decades to ex-

pire. The same "they," years later,
excised Margaret's heart & left it
pumping blue blood on the palace floor
across which they'd already dragged her beloved Peter.

Victory

"My Lord Archbishop, you may put away your books,"
Margaret was said to have said.
That eminent personage was withering at his desk
in a circle of black lamplight when the heart-

broken princess flew in upon him
like one of Group Captain Peter Townsend's planes
during the Battle of Britain—these now revolve
as in a mobile above a stillborn child's bed.

Portraits

At Buckingham, the Queen shuts lights in empty rooms,
such disillumination pleasing. Her skin seems
softer & more protective, shadows strengthen her,
ancestors are grateful & can sleep outside the glare

of wasted energy, or study. Now history
subsides, every glitch or serious sin or heresy
reduced to the memories of soporific books.
Another switch, *plish*, those lives go dark.

Spots in Time

When asked by the Shah of Iran
which political party best supported the Queen,
Elizabeth could only stutter—neither one
above the other, royal politics is oxymoronic, . . .

& then the Shah blurred, chandeliers fuzzed
while Lilibet was a girl again. At Windsor,
she stood by a pool of gold & pearl fish
who lipped surface, rippling clouds in her hair.

Figure

On tour in the far reaches of Commonwealth—
Malawi, Zambia, Botswana & Kenya—Elizabeth,
this configured evening, progressed along
a reception line when one village chief was heard

to whisper to another, "My God,
the Queen is a woman!" Had the man imagined
the royal personage naked, & been shocked?
My God, the Queen is a symbol with breasts & buttocks!

Intruder

Fagan crouched in darkness, then ascended
a drainpipe, entered a first-floor window,
took off his sandals & socks, climbed stairs,
& padded about until he found

his sovereign's boudoir. The Queen sat bolt upright
in her four-poster as, for a quarter-hour,
his hand dripping blood, they conversed
about his problems. Try getting to her now.

Notre Dame

President Reagan & Queen Elizabeth on horseback
for a quiet ride in Windsor Great Park,
but the Gipper pauses to have his picture taken
by the White House press. This annoys the Queen,

as does the President's breaking protocol by
sometimes riding ahead of her.
For too long, he's been a cowboy,
she mutters, & a Catholic football player.

Watergate

Richard Nixon at lunch at Buckingham Palace
places his waterglass atop a fork. Water
spills onto the Queen's knee. "O bother,"
she says. A servant tries to pat her dry with lace,

while Tricky Dick blithely scopes the place,
cases it in case he'll ask J. Edgar
to bug it. In any case, his nonplussed puss
belies delight at the wet royal pain-in-the-posterior.

The Queen's Philatelic Collection

"How about a headless stamp?" the sucker asked,
but the Queen's profile or portrait had always been
part of the design, displacing even *Great Britain*.
Elizabeth's displeasure was noted & passed on,

the Postmaster General lived to eat his question,
the royal collection breathed relief,
a rose arose on each replicated cheek,
a million Elizabeths went winkwinkwinkwinkwink.

Rhyme & Reason

A. N. Wilson argues that "the Sovereign might survive
without having a reason to survive."
A queen or king might be a rubber stamp
with face & crown a rubber stamp

for laws or acts of the houses of Parliament.
Why should the monarchy survive, Parliament
might well ask, without having a reason,
unless in the asking, we unreason that reason? . . .

Fidei Defensor

By the time you read this, maybe (but I doubt it)
an English woman will have been ordained.
Both Monarch & Parliament would have had to ratify
this outbreak of decadent modern temper, & Di

would have had to model ordination fashions,
& Charles would have had to pontificate on women
& the rural health, & the Queen, O the Queen
would have to cross her legs with each communion.

Backbench

Bagehot called George III a "meddling maniac."
Monarchs need be mute except to warn,
or to encourage, or when consulted, & then
the royal voice must be a blooming twig, not stick,

so what's the scoop with Charlie bloke
& his doodlebug opinions
on farms & architecture's frozen music?
He's better talking dirty on the phone.

A Dream of Berries

A picnic on a heathered hill at Balmoral,
spring beginning to bloom, the pines'
deep winter gloom only memory.
A picnic, but this once we'll see

no one on the spread blankets
or at the checkered tables on which the sun
seems to rest its watery purple body in relief.
A bear breathes sunny dust in its den.

Avalanche

Charles dreams snowblocks hurtling toward him,
then over him, but forming a dome
to protect his head. Then all is still,
crystalline, glittering & dark, but warm,

the illuminated Alps somehow small
as a paperweight in his gauntleted hands
into which he stares until
the snow gives up the body of his friend.

Snow

Charles walks through London snow as if
anybody else, a Cossack hat half
hiding his face, his ears covered
by snow-covered fur, the city muffled,

& not even one bodyguard to protect him.
Here he is, then, within that fable
of royalty who desert their golden rooms
to wander as commoners among their people,

Time

in search of something they've been lost without,
but what? Today, Charles remains intent
on walking block after block, content
to kick through deepening slush in gutters,

through sidewalk snow. It will be a long time
before his instinct tells him it's time
to begin wending his way back, time
to identify himself at the gates of Buckingham

The Question

as HRH Charles, Prince of Wales, Etc. Later,
tea will be brought to him, its vapor
reminding him of smoke puffing from grates,
of horses' breath in the Christmas air

through which, for now, he strides this London
of Shakespeare & Dickens, Doyle & . . . that librarian . . .
Larkin—these carried from bookshops like spirits
immortal for the common thing they'd written.

Epiphany

Charles attended the opening of "Art That Inflames"—
paintings & weird *sui generis* sculptures
that fill their space with noise, pain, violence,
colors whose edges sear the eye, toxic sludge

leaking from punctured eyeballs, bulbous penises
(or so they seemed to him) crawling with roaches,
Bach's head impaled on London Bridge
as "Toccata in D Minor" reverberates like a marriage.

The Tan Transcendentalist

After the best week's vacation of his life,
the young Prince wrote his hosts a thank-you:
"Every drop of water, every gamma ray of sunlight,
each particle of sand, every glutinous drop of oil

was stored away in the luckiest of brain cells."
Even as he penned these words, the oil,
sunlight, & water were miscible in his mind,
& his own royal soul fused with Oversoul.

Duchy: The Flowers

The Prince visited a flower farm
where daffodils were being cut.
The new tenant pointed out
the erosion of a cliff at field's end. . . .

"Nothing we can do," the tenant said.
"Except," said Charles, "watch your field
slowly disappear." (Yellow bloom.)
"*Your* field," his tenant reminded him.

Vocation

Charles lay long abed watching the hum
of an electric heater,
its orange coils, eight or ten
glowing vertical strands. . . .

He wondered how metal could focus &
conduct such scattered energy
into power. From childhood's hour, only
diffuse passionate light in him. . . .

Round Trip

Charles read a book whose poems
were each eight lines,
two quatrains,
usually rhymed. The poems reminded him

of double-decker buses, & he could ride them
above traffic no matter what
their subject,
usually Di & himself as repellent forces, or fictions.

One Hand Clapping

Charles admires a painting by Edward Browner
of a cricket match at Oxford—spires
in the background, in the foreground a green field
focusing on the wicket as a kind of grail.

Called, enigmatically, "House of Commons,"
Browner's vision suspends an early evening
in balances of shadows & arrested motions
Charles carries with him like his koan.

Death

Charles logged 500 hrs. at the controls
of a Wessex 5 double-engined copter,
then commanded a coastal minehunter
patrolling from the Scottish Isles

to the Irish Sea & English Channel
to the North Sea where, in tidal swells,
he watched a body pass before his bow, familiar,
under its own dead power.

Schornsteinfeger

In Hannover Di watched a chimney sweep
walking high above the street, & was reminded
of a scarecrow, wire bristles & tophat,
baggy trousers. That night, someone

walked the gables of her dreams while the sun
colored its horizon an auspicious rose-gold.
Whether she knew it or not, the sweep symbolized
the best of luck, & harvest, especially for brides.

Ocean

Probing her first jewelry box, Di found
a pin she'd almost forgotten—round,
a pane of mother-of-pearl crossed
with two silver strips embossed

with her initials, D . S . She pressed
this modest gift to her lips & kissed it
before her mind could salvage
its particular occasion before marriage

The Ravening

buried her body in a shroud
weighted down with lead.
Mother-of-pearl & silver,
but she could not remember,

but then she did—as though a shark
had brushed against her, had left her,
but now turned toward her again, one black-
flashed eyejewel of nightmare.

Time's Body

Di dreamed a window in her breast,
a field of stars. The feeling was like being
on *The Enterprise*'s bridge in "Star Trek"
with that family whose patriarch was Captain Kirk,

& looking toward the future into which
their ship cut at warpspeed like
an arrow from a primal mind's quiver
through the diamonds of a crushed tiara.

Clotheshorse

Di's duds await her for an early breakfast.
Notes for her brief speech are ready & thrice-read.
She can almost smell her words, the tea & pastries.
Her hosts will introduce her as a saint.

Time now to rest, maybe an hour's telly, maybe
"Hoss" Cartwright, the jovial fat brother in "Bonanza,"
the Old West where on their Ponderosa
a family of lonely men are sometimes happy.

Spring Song

Diana at her maiden's best,
boo-hoo, boo-hoo,
broke the heart in Everyman's breast,
you too, you too,

tu-whit, tu-whoo,
come live with me & be my love
& we will all the pleasures prove
my little English cuckoo. . . .

Seat Selection

Charles fastened his eyes on a wingtip rivet.
Below, ground drifted behind him like the past,
a thousand years of it.
Now his mind was a wing fixed on one thought,

that bitch, as it cut sunlight through cloud wisps
& regrets. She would never not relegate him
to his place in history, she whose only perspective
was from the cockpit.

Cortez

When I was a kid I called Cannon's Groceries
in old Nesconset, spoke low as I could,
asked if they had Prince Albert in a can.
"Yes," they said. "Then let him out," I yelled,

& hung up, & laughed with my friends.
I can still see that red tobacco tin
picturing the bearded prince, "Bertie,"
who cried at his forced accession, cried piteously.

Cortez II

When I was a kid I called Cannon's,
a store in old Nesconset, asked
if they had Prince Albert in a can.
"Yes," they said. "Then let him out," I yelled,

& hung up, & laughed with my friends.
I can still see that red tobacco tin
picturing that prince, Victoria's beloved husband
who rusts underground in a million replications.

Northwest Royal Mounted Police

When I was ten I called a grocery store
in old Nesconset & asked whoever answered,
"Do you have Prince Albert in a can?"
"Yes," she said. "Then let him out before

he suffocates," I yelled, & slammed the phone down.
I can still see the red tobacco tin that pictured
the bearded prince, Victoria's son, who loved
screwing around as much as anyone.

December 11, 1937

On abdication morning, writes Anne Edwards,
"a funeral pall hovered over London."
Among the masses who gathered outside Buckingham
was a poet I met twenty years ago in Oxford—

he said he couldn't sleep, arrived at first gray light,
held to iron grillework & repeatedly
heard in his mind the mysterious audition,
Dulce et decorum est pro patria mori.

Retrospect

As though his & Diana's marriage had meant
that Adam & Eve had returned to the garden—
Charles had to laugh at romantic countryfolk
but then remembered how the event evoked

such strange stirrings in his own genitals & breast
of indescribable essence of honor, patriotism,
the return home, crown & loins & blonde hair
commingling in vows of the kingdom to come.

Tent Shadows

Charles woke to a few instants of not knowing
who or where he was. The who came first—
the Prince of Wales. Then the where—a forest,
no, a jungle, Tanganyika. He'd been dreaming,

dreaming deeply of a woman whose identity
wavered, or fused between/among Camilla, Di,
& the Queen. A dream, he realized, was a safari
on which you carried every woman in your life.

Gift

In Edinburgh a couple starting up a business
cut clocks into pieces of Scottish rock.
One clock looked like a chunk
taken from Balmoral, the Prince remarked.

That timepiece now keeps its one grimace
in a warehouse filled with kitch—
its hands askew, its face
a royal blue wedding of the Prince & Princess.

Lion

In the Kalahari Charles saw a lion, old,
alone, its mane rusted. It had left its pride
to live its death. It walked
as though in meditation over a dune

into the Prince's chest, a caution,
but of what? The African sunset framed him,
monarch in a trance of time,
unheralded, soon dead, supreme.

Mirror

Describing taking an exam, Charles said:
"I had the feeling that I was writing
on a mirror and my pen was being held
from the other side!" This feeling

that something was writing him, something
knowing what he was thinking,
struck him as "a most curious sensation."
As *you* move here in knowing anticipation . . .

Subject Matter

Di at Princess Grace's funeral
kept thinking of the white poodle
given to the actress decades before by Cary Grant
as a wedding present,

& of something he'd replied when critics dismissed
motion pictures that were fluff & glitz:
"Is a garbage can any more real
than Buckingham Palace?"

Golf

Charles in the U.S. for the Ryder, 1995.
I saw him stand on the players' side /
of the ropes, watched his body language
as he leaned European drives & putts toward,

then into the . . . cup. This was Rochester, New York,
corporate home of Eastman Kodak whose stock
would have flashed had the woman who tripped
Charles's shutter—or so we thought—

The Celebrant

showed up. Now, with future knowledge,
I wonder how heartsick he & Di were that week,
& what was on the Prince's mind who stood
in his rain-slicker to say, "Well struck,"

"Nick," "sublime, Colin," as his homeboys
came from behind to beat the favored Yanks
in the last days on the last holes of Oak Hill,
Dunsinane come to Birnham Wood.

Marriage Emblem, 1996

The QE2 plowed into Lisbon harbor Sunday
with a dead 60-foot whale pinned to her bow.
Obtuse to criticism, Captain Stanley (no relation)
shrugged off the incident saying, "It's just

one of those things, like running over a cat."
When workers cut away the ripe 15-ton cetacean,
one mentioned Moby Dick, another asked "Whose dick?"
& gulls flew in for a feast unfit for a queen.

Crime of the Century

Di knew what to make of that O.J. travesty.
Enough said, even to herself, & maybe
too much. The blonde wife's head
had been almost severed

by the brutal bastard who'd dripped blood,
his & hers, from L.A. to Westminster Abbey
where someone less frightfully butchered
prayed in a pew this day, & shuddered.

For Want of a Crowbar

"There were three of us in the marriage,
so it got crowded,"
Di said.
She'd no way to exert leverage,

no way to pry mistress Camilla's head
from their pillow,
or torso
from the isosceles of their marriage bed.

Fashion

When she was a girl, Di dyed
a yellow sweater forest green,
& she was proud, so very proud
when the sweater turned out beautifully,

but why today while signing papers
does she remember her dyed creation?
Yellow to green, now this unknown region
of divorce in colors of grief, in motley.

First Edition

Di's favorite nonentity in *Alice in Wonderland*
was the Cheshire cat who seemed to be there,
& then wasn't, but was, but where?
She mimicked Tenniel's feline in a mirror,

but once, when she stared for too long, seemed
. . . .
to disappear. O how this frightened her
into staying conscious as she grinned. . . .

Illumination

Diana nodded when Mother Teresa told her,
"To heal others, you yourself have to suffer."
Right now, she felt like the leather Bunyan
at Kensington, journeying to Celestial City

but half disbound. Teresa's wrists,
she noticed, were vellum on which was illumined
the story of Father Damien among the lepers.
"Diana, turn this way," the paparazzi shouted.

Ecology

The faces on my Charles & Di bookmark
wear away, the blue-stained leather
cracks & flakes in afterweather.
Charles's nose, Di's lips, the heart

enclosing them—all disappear.
But everything must go somewhere,
in this commoner house of ours
or in the castles of the Windsors.

The Monarchy in the Next Millennium

A new species discovered, visible
to the naked eye, an animal
that lives on a lobster's lip,
shaped like a billowing ship

out of the days of pirates & the bounding main.
Symbiotic nor parasitic, its connection
with its crustacean is like nothing known before,
a condom filled with rubies & a claw.

Ugly American

The one time I stood by Victoria's Monument
& looked over at Buckingham Palace,
I thought the packed-dirt courtyard—
though swept clean & sprinkled—evidence

of England in decline. I'd expected grass,
as at the White House. What's not to venerate
in a western lawn kept kempt
& homogeneous with poisons & bad taste?

Triptych Misc.

Freesias are Di's favorite bloom.
Charles treasures books inscribed to him by Churchill.
"Mr. Gorilla" lives in Di's bedroom—
"He keeps an eye on me," she says with a smile.

Charles treasures books inscribed to him by Van der Post,
who acknowledges the Prince's "meditative heart."
Di likes to burn jasmine-scented candles.
Hanging from her mantle are several

Convertible

signed ballet shoes (she grew too tall
to be a ballerina). American Robert Heindel
is her favorite artist. A shredding machine
keeps busy above her waste bin when,

twice each day, the mail arrives
from Tunis & Zanzibar & Zanesville, Ohio.
Charles's seat is stiff in his polo saddle.
Di prides her skill behind the wheel, . . .

The Sun Never Sets

& that things go round & again go round
has sort of a classical sound,
said the poet Wallace Stevens who never once
got to France to mellifluize his French *in situ*—

his wife, Elsie, was the model for Liberty
on the U.S. Mercury dime, which was silver.
What we make of our own or others' lives, O
this empire survives on sounds, & velocity.

Hymen

Kaiser Wilhelm (for whom I was named)
once remarked, "Monarchy is like virginity:
once lost, you can't restore it."
There's good reason for me to be ashamed

of my irrelevant parenthetical, but it came to me.
Of course, I could revise, but in the spirit
of my subject, I'll be wilhelmed
if I'll change it, so these eight lines are lost.

Ars Genealogica

I was named for Wilhelm, my father's brother,
killed in Holland, 1941, foot soldier
of the *Wehrmacht*. He was named for the Kaiser,
Queen Victoria's grandson, d. 1941.

I was born November 1, two months before 1941,
& christened "Willi," the Kaiser's
& my dead uncle's nickname. That soldier & I—
only a poem's throw to the Queen, & Di!

Meditation & Return

The coronation coach's panels are painted with seascapes.
For now, we'll forget the year & stare
into the painted waters. At the mouth of the Thames,
a stylized whale spouts; at Loch Ness, a serpent rises

& peers about. Deep in its black pupil
resides its secret that goes back to Grendel.
With me, swim through waterspout & maelstrom
to reach our warrior king, god save him.

Circus

When Charles saw the photos of Fergie's lover
sucking her toes, he first thought of his mother—
during the *annus horribilis* the old lady
had reeled from marriage splits & Windsor fire—

then laughed the human laugh of *Schadenfreude*.
For all he cared, the Duchess of York could
(& maybe should) charge admission as she
diddled her Texan in Piccadilly.

Miscarriage

Late in September 1983 Di became pregnant,
but lost this child.
The Queen had called for champagne, & drank
health to the child,

but the Princess lost perhaps the daughter
she'd yearned for.
But now, soon after, she was pregnant again
with the "spare,"

Absentee Father

Harry. Di's back ached, her thin legs
tired easily, stairs
took her breath, her clothes fit like tents of the Tuareg,
desert wanderers,

but this second son reached full term
& Di birthed him
for himself, his brother, his country
& the Queen.

Georgic

"After all I've done for that fucking family"—
Diana, intercepted on the phone.
Through her, those musty bores were "cool" again,
& she, well *she*

wouldn't be treated like a surrogate
who dropped babies on the throne
& then retired to cows & grass.
The Windsors could kiss her royal American.

Divorce Astronomy

Di danced with the general who ran
America's first war in the desert.
The commander wore a tux, she a gown
spangled with gold stars & red velvet

half moons. Next day, at a cancer benefit,
she spoke of "new, improved life." Britain's
"princess forsaken"—one paper's epithet—
all Washington in her constellation.

Herstory

For his summer palace above the Black Sea,
a German prince planted a Japanese garden,
then imported thousands of butterfly chrysalides
so that his flowers "might not be lonely."

His garden cascaded down his cliffs
like Di's dream wherein she rems:
frail winged jewels waver in seawind
in waves wherein a princess flounders.

Working Jigsaw Puzzles

Queen Elizabeth starts not with edge or corner,
but with the most vibrant color.
She does this without thinking, just letting
her hands move over the pieces

like manta rays
waving their fins, her fingers.
Time passes, she fits the first color together,
& all is possible in the House of Windsor.

Rasputin Box

For their wedding, Charles & Di received
(via one grand duchess or another)
a Romanov heirloom, 'an amethystine agate
and silver gilt snuff box with ruby lift.'

Charles, press your finger to the ruby, & lift.
Notice the box's false bottom, a mirror
into which the mad monk himself once stared,
under which he hid, for you, a vial of his blood.

Riddle

What happened? What *really* happened,
Charles wonders. One scandal after another—
his, Fergie's, Di's—coming together
like a curse on the Windsors. But what

did happen, where did everything begin?
All he'd wanted was to survive those bloody years
of early schooling, to be & to father the future king.
Is the cosmos fraught with counter-force?

Fate

the yang-yin corrective for pride & power,
or did there lurk a single fuck-up gene
in the long history of the royal line?
Was this a philosophical question on the origins

of indiscretion & stupidity, or merely
chicken & egg musings? What really happened
to muddle & sully his life like this, he
who wanted to work, respect his place, & be happy?

Hygiene

At Harare Charles visited a privy
he thought nifty—
the plastic chimney pipe rose ten feet high,
& trapped flies,

& bore smells of the foul pit
out of the hut
by way of updraught, like a story carried
by a tabloid.

1948

The day he was born, Trafalgar's fountain
bubbled blue for Charles, heir to the throne.
A month later, water from the River Jordan
baptized him. That year, tons of snoek

(a fish held in disdain) came to market
as food was rationed in all Britain,
with petrol unavailable. A nation in decline
took to the Prince like Henry VIII to communion.

Charles: The Unaccountable

"Deep in the soul of mankind
there is a reflection as on the surface
of a mirror-calm lake of the beauty
and harmony of the universe.

"But so often that reflection is obscured
and ruffled by unaccountable storms.
So much depends, I think, on how
each of us is introduced to

The Reflection

"and made aware of that reflection
within us. So, I believe
we have a duty to our children
to develop this awareness,

"for it seems to me that it is only through
individual inner peace
and the outward manifestation
of that reflection,

Living Art

"that we can ever hope to attain
the kind of peace in this world
for which so many yearn.
We must strive if we can

"to make living
into an art itself, although it will
always remain
a tremendous struggle."

Advice

"She should get a beautiful female lover,"
says a gossip of Di's future.
"After Buckingham Palace," says another,
"Di needs a sex life, and central heating,

"and maybe a prosthesis for her posture."
In any case, the pundits are agreeing:
the marriage was mythic & a lie,
now Di must be her own excuse for being.

Boy King

Five hundred years ago, this movement
in the tomb of Tutankhamen:
a gold-leafed chair collapses, dust
swirls up in cerement darkness, then

the long settling of motes. In this way, a poem
breaks down into the gold & dust of time,
atom by atom. But the masked self
bears eternal witness to its hieroglyph.

Job: Double Spondee

Students of The Prince's Trust
practice job interviews.
One young biker's hair is purple,
her cleavage blooms tattoos—

she wouldn't make a royal impression, youse
wouldn't suppose—
but the Prince tosses in his sleep,
& four gold rings pierce his nose.

Prisoners

March, 1997, days after meeting Di,
Nelson Mandela said he was "still trembling."
For her part, the Princess was "absolutely thrilled"
to have met this man whom Robens Island

could not break. Di was almost herself again,
in fact more so than she'd ever been,
radiant for the Nobel president
(who dreamt South Africa as ebony as she).

Baglady

Shielding her face with her purse:
"Why don't you rape someone else?"—
Di shouted at several paparazzi.
She once flipped the royal finger

to a photographer who'd crowded her
once too often. Mother Teresa of Calcutta
laughed when she read this in the papers,
but prayed this daughter win her poverty.

Albatross

Its wings longest on earth since Pterodactyl,
the flying reptile. Now to us here
this mariner glides over the whitecaps,
a thought of ocean we've had before,

correspondence of feathered light
& the Crown Jewels, its eyes
in their wine-dark timeless seeing
free of us for its killing. . . .

About the Author

William Heyen was born in Brooklyn, New York, in 1940. He is currently Professor of English and Poet in Residence at the State University of New York at Brockport, his undergraduate alma mater. His graduate degrees are from Ohio University. A former Senior Fulbright Lecturer in American Literature in Germany, he has won awards and fellowships from NEA, the Guggenheim Foundation, *Poetry* magazine, and the American Academy and Institute of Arts and Letters. His work has appeared in *Harper's*, *The New Yorker*, *American Poetry Review*, *TriQuarterly*, *The Southern Review*, *The Nation*, *The Ontario Review*, and in many anthologies. William Heyen is the editor of *American Poets in 1976* and *The Generation of 2000: Contemporary American Poets*. His books of poetry include *Depth of Field*, *Noise in the Trees* (an American Library Association Notable Book of the Year), *The Swastika Poems*, *Long Island Light: Poems and a Memoir*, *Erika: Poems of the Holocaust*, *Ribbons: The Gulf War*, *Pterodactyl Rose: Poems of Ecology*, and *The Host: Selected Poems 1965-1990*. *Crazy Horse in Stillness*, published by BOA Editions, Ltd., was awarded the 1997 Small Press Book Award for Poetry. Heyen's *Pig Notes & Dumb Music: Prose on Poetry* has also recently appeared from BOA.

Acknowledgments

Some poems in this collection stemmed from my recent reading in newspapers and magazines. Books that sparked poems here include Ross Benson's *Charles: The Untold Story* (1993); Lady Colin Campbell's *Diana in Private* (1992); Jonathan Dimbleby's *The Princess of Wales: A Biography* (1994); Anne Edwards' *Royal Sisters: Queen Elizabeth II and Princess Margaret* (1990); Roland Flamini's *Sovereign: Elizabeth II and the Windsor Dynasty* (1991); Andrew Morton's *Diana: Her True Story* (1992); Anna Pasternak's *Princess in Love* (1994); Richard Tomlinson's *Divine Right: The Inglorious Survival of British Royalty* (1994); James Whitaker's *Diana vs Charles: Royal Blood Feud* (1993); A. N. Wilson's *The Rise & Fall of the House of Windsor* (1993); and Lauren van der Post's *Feather Fall* (1994), edited by Jean-Marc Rottiez.

Index of Poems

BOA EDITIONS, LTD.

AMERICAN POETS CONTINUUM SERIES